SEASONS

FALL

Stephanie Turnbull

Published by Smart Apple Media
P.O. Box 1329
Mankato, MN 56002

Printed in the United States of America,
at Corporate Graphics in North Mankato, Minnesota.

Designed by Hel James
Edited by Mary-Jane Wilkins

Library of Congress Cataloging-in-Publication Data

Turnbull, Stephanie.
 Fall / by Stephanie Turnbull.
    p. cm. -- (The seasons)
 Includes bibliographical references and index.
 Summary: "Uses photos to help describe the changes
that happen to the weather, plants, and animals in fall.
Mentions the holidays and events that usually occur in
fall months"--Provided by publisher.
 Audience: Grades K-3.
 ISBN 978-1-59920-849-7 (hbk., library bound : alk.
paper)
 1. Autumn--Juvenile literature. I. Title.
 QB637.7.T87 2013
 508.2--dc23
                                    2012004120

Photo acknowledgements
t = top, b = bottom
page 1 odze/Shutterstock; page 3 iStockphoto/
Thinkstock; 5 background iStockphoto/Thinkstock,
inset Poznyakov/Shutterstock; 6 Paul Aniszewski/
Shutterstock; 7 Ingram Publishing/Thinkstock;
8 iStockphoto/Thinkstock; 9 Stockbyte/Thinkstock;
10 Ron Chapple Studios/Thinkstock; 11t SAJE/
Shutterstock, b iStockphoto/Thinkstock;
12 iStockphoto/Thinkstock; b Medioimages/
Photodisc; 14 iStockphoto/Thinkstock;
15 CreativeNature.nl/Shutterstock; 16-17 Myotis/
Shutterstock; 18 iStockphoto/Thinkstock;
19 Tom Grundy/Shutterstock; 20 JeniFoto/
Shutterstock; 21 iStockphoto/Thinkstock;
22 background Shunsuke Yamamoto Photography/
Thinkstock; 23t Hemera/Thinkstock, b Kai Wong/
Shutterstock
Cover Ingram Publishing/Thinkstock

DAD0505
042012
9 8 7 6 5 4 3 2 1

Contents

It's Fall!

Fat orange
pumpkins are
ripe and ready.

Shorter Days

Our fall months are September, October, and November.

The sun comes up later every morning and sets earlier every evening.

Sunlight *is* weaker,
so fall can be chilly.
Dress warmly!

Wet and Dry

Many fall mornings are misty. Glittering drops of dew cover grass, leaves, and spider webs.

Some days are wild, wet, and windy.

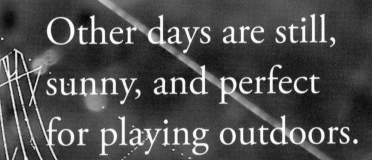

Other days are still,
sunny, and perfect
for playing outdoors.

Taking a Break

Plants stop growing in fall. Some die, but others have roots alive underground.

These flowers bloom in fall, then die back.

Leaves turn
golden yellow,
flaming red, or
rusty brown.

Leaves Everywhere!

Gusts of wind send dry leaves fluttering to the ground.

Winged seeds whirl
through the air.
Next year these
may start growing
into new trees.

Fat mushrooms sprout
in damp piles of leaves.

Fruit and Food

Raspberries and blackberries are fat and juicy in the fall.

Spiky green fruits on horse chestnut trees protect the big, glossy seeds inside.

It's time for farmers to gather their crops. This is called a harvest.

Munch, Munch

Animals gobble all the nuts, seeds, and berries they can find. Winter is coming and soon there will be less to eat. Squirrels store extra nuts in safe places.

Bye Bye!

Some animals don't wait for winter—they leave instead! These geese are flying south to warmer places. Their journey may take weeks.

They will come back in spring.

Yawn...

Many animals find safe places to sleep through the winter.

Mice curl up tightly in cozy nests.

Insects such as butterflies look for cracks or piles of logs to hide in.

Bats hang upside down
in quiet caves.

Fall Fun

Many fall festivals celebrate harvest time and all the crops that have grown.

Halloween is a time to dress up and have a spooky party with your friends!

Did You Know...?

When we have fall, it is spring in the southern half of the world.

Trees called evergreens don't lose their leaves in fall.

Every fall, birds called
Arctic terns fly from
the North Pole
all the way to
the South Pole!

At Chinese harvest
festivals, people
eat sweet pastries
called mooncakes.

Useful Words

crops
Plants such as wheat and corn that are grown by farmers for food.

fall
The time of year, called a season, after summer and before winter

dew
Water in the air that gathers on cool surfaces at night.

roots
Plant parts that store water and food from soil to keep the plant alive.

Index